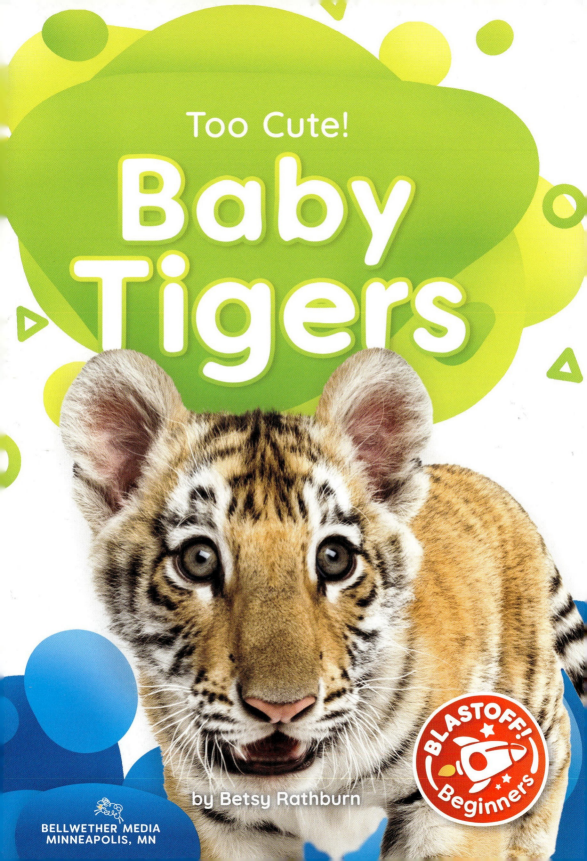

Too Cute!
Baby Tigers

by Betsy Rathburn

BELLWETHER MEDIA
MINNEAPOLIS, MN

Blastoff! Beginners

Blastoff! Beginners are developed by literacy experts and educators to meet the needs of early readers. These engaging informational texts support young children as they begin reading about their world. Through simple language and high frequency words paired with crisp, colorful photos, Blastoff! Beginners launch young readers into the universe of independent reading.

Sight Words in This Book

a	can	her	play	this
and	eat	in	she	to
are	for	is	the	two
at	get	it	them	with
big	have	look	they	

This edition first published in 2024 by Bellwether Media, Inc.

No part of this publication may be reproduced in whole or in part without written permission of the publisher. For information regarding permission, write to Bellwether Media, Inc., Attention: Permissions Department, 6012 Blue Circle Drive, Minnetonka, MN 55343.

Library of Congress Cataloging-in-Publication Data

Names: Rathburn, Betsy, author.
Title: Baby tigers / by Betsy Rathburn.
Description: Minneapolis, MN : Bellwether Media, Inc., 2024. | Series: Blastoff! Beginners. Too cute! | Includes bibliographical references and index. | Audience: Ages 4-7 | Audience: Grades K-1
Identifiers: LCCN 2023000130 (print) | LCCN 2023000131 (ebook) | ISBN 9798886874075 (library binding) | ISBN 9798886875959 (ebook)
Subjects: LCSH: Tiger--Infancy--Juvenile literature.
Classification: LCC QL737.C23 R38 2024 (print) | LCC QL737.C23 (ebook) | DDC 599.75613/92--dc23/eng/20230112
LC record available at https://lccn.loc.gov/2023000130
LC ebook record available at https://lccn.loc.gov/2023000131

Text copyright © 2024 by Bellwether Media, Inc. BLASTOFF! BEGINNERS and associated logos are trademarks and/or registered trademarks of Bellwether Media, Inc.

Editor: Rachael Barnes   Designer: Laura Sowers

Printed in the United States of America, North Mankato, MN.

Table of Contents

A Baby Tiger!	4
Life with Mom	6
Growing Up!	16
Baby Tiger Facts	22
Glossary	23
To Learn More	24
Index	24

A Baby Tiger!

Look at the baby tiger.
Hello, cub!

Life with Mom

Cubs are born in a **litter**. They have soft fur.

litter

They cuddle together.
They **nurse**.

cuddling

Mom carries them in her mouth. She keeps them safe.

They play and fight. They **pounce** and bite!

pounce

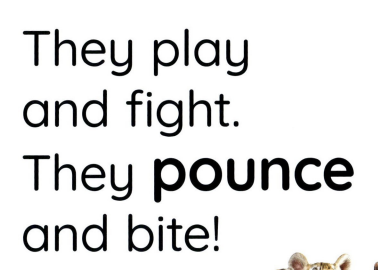

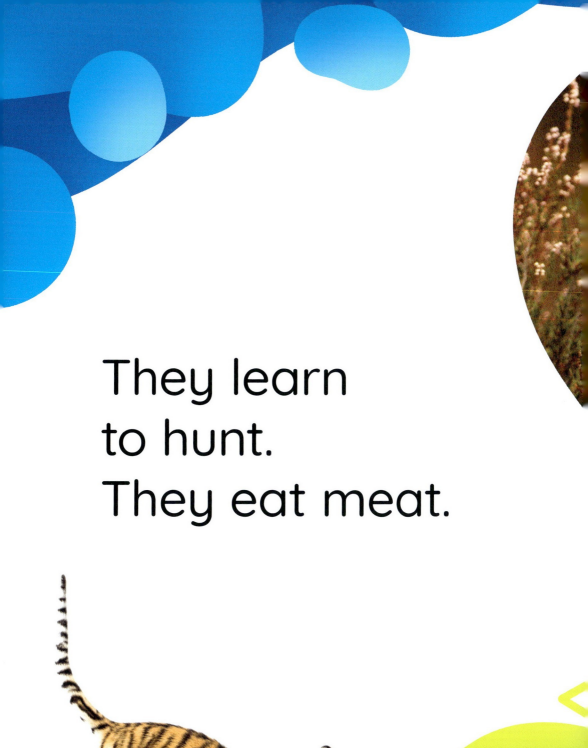

They learn to hunt.
They eat meat.

Growing Up!

Cubs grow. They get big teeth and claws.

claws

They stay with mom for two years.

This cub is grown.
It can live alone.
Bye, mom!

Baby Tiger Facts

Tiger Life Stages

cub   adult

A Day in the Life

nurse   play and fight   learn to hunt

22

Glossary

litter

a group of cubs born at the same time

nurse

to drink mom's milk

pounce

to jump

To Learn More

ON THE WEB

FACTSURFER

Factsurfer.com gives you a safe, fun way to find more information.

1. Go to www.factsurfer.com.

2. Enter "baby tigers" into the search box and click 🔍.

3. Select your book cover to see a list of related content.

Index

alone, 20	hunt, 14	pounce, 12
bite, 12	learn, 14	safe, 10
claws, 16	litter, 6	teeth, 16, 17
cuddle, 8	meat, 14	tiger, 4
eat, 14	mom, 10, 11, 18, 20	
fight, 12	nurse, 8, 9	
fur, 6	play, 12	
grow, 16, 20		

The images in this book are reproduced through the courtesy of: Eric Isselee, cover, pp. 3, 4, 4-5, 6, 12, 14, 22 (adult); Barbora Polivkova, pp. 6-7; dpa picture alliance archive/ Alamy, p. 8; cgwp.co.uk/ Alamy, pp. 8-9, 10-11; Edwin Butter, pp. 12-13; Dagmara Ksandrova, pp. 14-15; Michal Varga, p. 16; Anuradha Marwah, pp. 16-17; PhotocechCZ, pp. 18-19; ehtesham, p. 20; Martin Mecnarowski, pp. 20-21; Anan Kaewkhammul, p. 22 (cub); slowmotiongli, pp. 22 (nurse), 23 (nurse); Evgeniyqw, p. 22 (play and fight); Zaruba Ondrej, p. 22 (learn to hunt); Bogomolov Sergey, p. 23 (litter); Stanislav Duben, p. 23 (pounce).